Waldo, Tell Me About Christ

Waldo™ Series

Published by The Regina Press, Melville, New York 11747

ISBN 088271 470 8

Printed in Belgium

Waldo, Tell Me About Christ

by Hans Wilhelm

Regina Press
New York

It was a gray and wet Sunday afternoon. Michael felt very unhappy. Sad and lonely thoughts filled his mind as he watched the falling raindrops.

His best friend, Waldo,
tried very hard to cheer him up.
Nothing worked.
    "I wish someone understood
how I really feel," sighed Michael.

"Christ does," said Waldo gently.

Michael looked up at his friend. "Waldo, tell me about Christ," he said.

"Well," said Waldo, "I'll tell you about Him if you'll come for a walk with me."

"In this rain?" said Michael sadly.

"Why not?"

As Waldo helped Michael with his jacket and boots, he began to explain.

"You see, Michael, Christ is the son of God. He lived here on earth as Jesus of Nazareth. He taught people all about God and showed us how we should live and love each other."

"What does that have to do with the way I feel?" asked Michael.

"Well," said Waldo. "Because Christ lived on earth as Jesus, He can really understand you. As Jesus, He experienced all the hurts and all the sorrows that any person has ever had. He knows exactly how you feel because He has felt it, too."

"Can He help me feel better?"
asked Michael.

"Oh, yes," said Waldo. "He's also
called the Great Comforter. You can
tell Him about your troubles and ask
Him to help you. And, He will as
long as what you ask for is good
for you."

"What do you mean?"
asked Michael.

"Christ knows that sometimes
feeling a little pain or sadness can be
good for you because it helps you to
understand how other people feel.
It makes us better friends. Christ
suffered as Jesus. He was treated
very badly."

Suddenly a boy on a motor bike
whizzed by.

"Duck, Michael!" shouted
Waldo. "He's going right through
that puddle!"
    The two friends were drenched
and Michael was very angry.
    "That big bully!" cried Michael.

"I'm really mad at him," said Michael.

"Why don't you try to forgive him?" said Waldo as he shook himself dry. "Do you know, Michael, that Christ forgave all the people who hurt Him? He taught us that if we want to be happy, we should forgive the people who hurt us, too."

"Do you mean that I should forgive that bully for getting us all wet?"

"Yes," said Waldo, "if you want to feel happy again. Because if you don't, you will stay angry and upset."

"Well, forgiving isn't easy to do," said Michael.

"Come, Michael," laughed Waldo.
"The rain has stopped. Let's enjoy
the puddles!"

Michael followed Waldo as he
hopped from puddle to puddle.

"Wasn't Christ ever mad at
the people who hurt Him?"
asked Michael.

"No, never. He forgave every single
one. And He tells us to do the same."

"And if you hurt someone, Michael, even if it's a mistake, you should ask them to forgive you, too. Christ teaches us that."

Michael thought about his anger. He thought about Christ.

"Can I ask Christ to forgive me?" asked Michael quietly.

"Oh, yes," said Waldo. "Christ is with you. He is listening to you and He is always ready to forgive you. When you tell Him that you are sorry, He helps you to feel happy in your heart. Christ will show you all the beauty and joy that is around you and within you."

"Christ shows you how much God loves you. He wants to help you when you feel low or sad. He will pick you up when you stumble on your way and make mistakes. Christ is your very best friend, Michael."

"But Waldo," said Michael, "what about you?"

"I am your friend, Michael, but Christ is more so. He is with you always. He is leading you to God, our loving Father."

Michael felt happy. The rain clouds had gone away. His sad feelings had gone away too. He loved Waldo.

Waldo had introduced him to a wonderful new friend—someone who would always understand him. Christ would be with him forever.

Never would Michael be lonely again.